Flip for Comprehension

Emily Cayuso

Maupin House *by*
capstone
professional

Flip for Comprehension
by Emily Cayuso

Layout/Design by Michael Cuthbertson
Illustrations by Michael Cuthbertson & Josh Clark

Library of Congress Cataloging-in-Publication Data

Cayuso, Emily, 1954-
  Flip for comprehension / Emily Cayuso.
      p. cm.
  Includes bibliographical references.
  ISBN 978-0-929895-83-3 (pbk.)
  ISBN 0-929895-83-5 (pbk.)
  1. Reading comprehension. I. Title.
  LB1050.45.C39 2005
  372.47—dc22
                              2005007667

Also by Emily Cayuso:
Designing Teacher Study Groups: A Guide for Success
Dar la Vuelta a la Comprensión
Flip for Word Work
Flip for Non-Fiction Comprehension

Maupin House Publishing, Inc. by Capstone Professional
1710 Roe Crest Drive
North Mankato, MN 56003
888-262-6135
www.maupinhouse.com

Publishing Professional Resources that Improve Classroom Performance

Printed in China.
052014   008267

Table of Contents

(E) Expository
(N) Narrative
(B) Both

Table of Contents

(E) Expository
(N) Narrative
(B) Both

Introduction

Helping children develop, master, and use a variety of comprehension strategies to understand what they read is an important goal of comprehension instruction. As the Texas Education Agency 2000 points out, we as teachers must provide explicit instruction to assist children in developing a repertoire of comprehension strategies that they can use to become independent, strategic, and metacognitive readers.

This packet is designed to provide teachers with ready-to-use comprehension ideas that can be done before, during, or after the reading of both fiction and non-fiction texts. In addition, many of the ideas presented can be used in various classroom settings.

Guided Reading: The teacher can use these activities with small guided reading groups as an extension of questioning and comprehension work.

Literacy Centers: This packet can be a stand-alone Comprehension Center or enhance and extend the work in an existing center such as the Writing, Listening, or Independent Reading/ Library Center.

Literature Circles: Ideas presented in this packet can be used as a guide to facilitate discussion and/or structure written responses or projects for the group to work on and share.

Read Alouds: Many of the activities and strategies facilitate, enhance, and extend student understanding of the text read aloud.

Independent Reading: Use these activities as a conversation springboard during the "sharing time" that follows the independent reading. In addition, if the teacher holds one on one conferences during the reading time, the teacher is provided with a way to check how well a student understands text he has read independently.

I..troductio..

Independent Writing: The Reader's Response page is one of several pages that can be used as a springboard for student writing and then class sharing.

To ensure student success with *Flip for Comprehension*, it is important to model the strategy with the students first, then follow with enough teacher-guided practice before the student can be expected to apply the strategy and/or activity independently.

These strategies/activities can be written or done orally. They can be used to guide whole group discussion, or children can be asked to complete the activities independently in their reading journals or on chart or construction paper. Likewise, the activities can be done in student pairs or small cooperative groups.

The ideas in this packet are not grouped in any particular format. As you use the Table of Contents as a quick reference guide, you will notice that there are ideas that can be used only with expository texts (e.g., "KWL Chart," "Expository Text Questions," "Retelling Important Informational Facts") and those that only can be used with narrative texts (e.g., "Narrative Story Structure," "Story Map," "Character Web"). Yet, because many ideas presented here can be used interchangeably with both types of texts, it becomes very difficult to categorize them all. You will need to look at the idea, the type of text your students are currently reading, and the particular comprehension needs you want to address. Perhaps your teacher's guide suggests an idea similar to one/s you find here. You may also find that certain stories naturally lend themselves to a particular activity. However you make your selections, remember that developing a repertoire of good comprehension strategies for all readers is the goal.

How to Use this Packet

- **Use this packet with a small group, whole class, or as part of an independent center.**

- **Stand the packet up like a tent to the page you want your students to work on.**

- **Insert any other information needed directly onto the page using sticky notes or cover-up tape.**

- **Model with your students how to successfully complete the activity.**

- **Provide the necessary materials to complete the activity.**

Author's Purpose

- What was the author's purpose in writing this text?

- In your reading journal or on a sheet of paper explain in your own words what you think the author's purpose was and why.

- Use any clues from your text to help support your answer.

Beginning, Middle, and End

- **Fold a sheet of paper into three sections.**

- **On the top of each section write the words "Beginning," "Middle," and "End."**

- **Write about and draw what happened in your story at those points.**

Beginning	Middle	End

Cause and Effect

- **Take a piece of paper and divide it in half.**

- **Write "Cause" on one side and "Effect" on the other.**

- **Find as many cause and effect relationships that happened in the text and put them in the chart.**

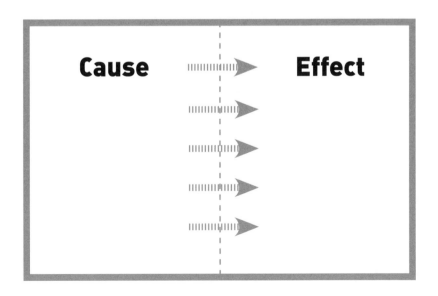

Character Chart

- **Make a character chart like the one below.**

- **Draw and write about the main character/s.**

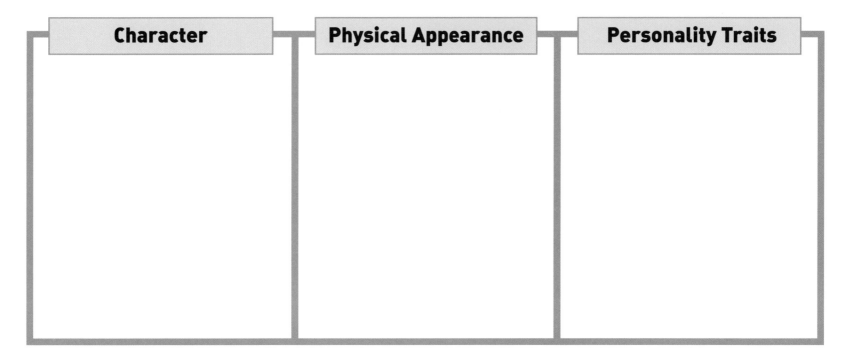

Character	Physical Appearance	Personality Traits

Character Fact and Opinion

- **Write three facts about the main character in your story.**

- **Write three opinions about the main character in your story.**

- **Draw a picture of the main character.**

Facts	Opinions	Picture

Character Talk

- **Draw a picture of the two main characters.**

- **Draw a speech bubble over each character.**

- **Fill in the speech bubble with words they might be saying to each other based on the events of the story.**

Character Web

- **Make a character web about the main character in your story.**

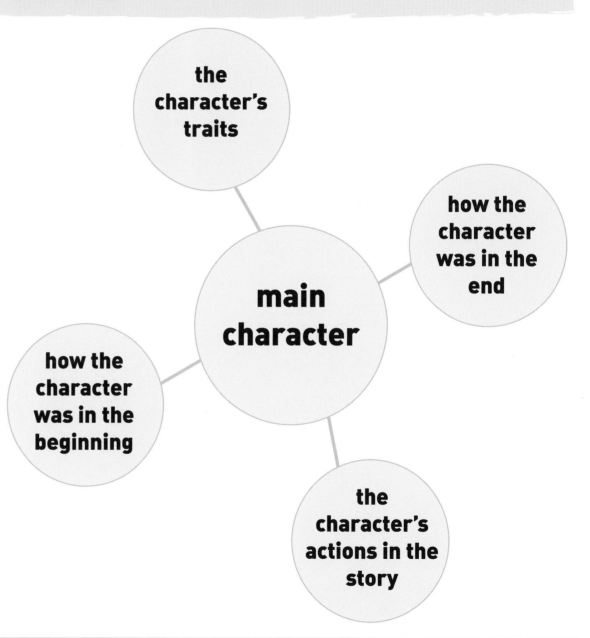

the character's traits

how the character was in the end

main character

how the character was in the beginning

the character's actions in the story

Charting the Chapters

- **Make a grid like this one.**

- **In each box write the chapter number and one or two sentences that summarize the important information in that chapter.**

Compare and Contrast

- **Make a Venn diagram comparing two characters, events, places, things, or other information from the text.**

- **In the center section, write what is the same about both.**

Cycle of Events

● **Recreate this graphic and fill it in with the important events from the text.**

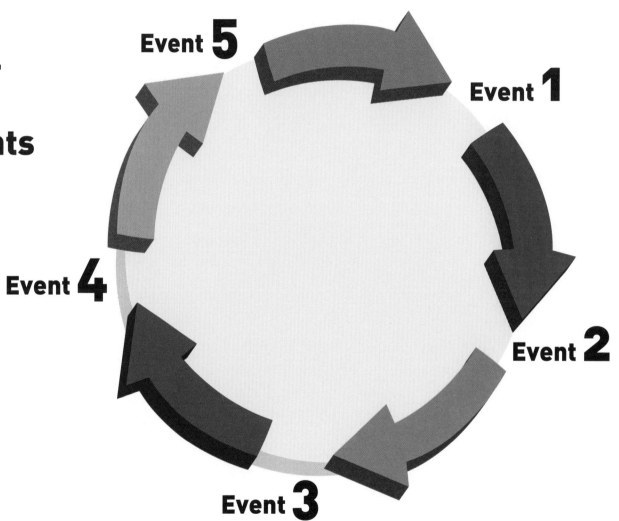

Event **5**

Event **1**

Event **2**

Event **3**

Event **4**

Direct Reading Thinking Activity

- Make a chart like the one on the next page.

- For every page your teacher writes on the chart, make a prediction about what you think will happen next in the text. Write it down.

- Use what you know about the text so far and your own understanding of the context of the story to make your prediction.

- After you read on, check to see if your prediction was right. Write down what actually happened in the story.

DRTA Chart

	What I think will happen	**What really happened**
Page _____		
Page _____		
Page _____		
Page _____		

Discovery

- **Write down three things that you discovered from the text that you didn't know before.**

- **Why were they new discoveries for you?**

Expository Text Questions

Answer these questions about your expository text:

- **What new words did you learn? Explain in your own words what they mean.**

- **What was the text mainly about?**

- **What new things did you learn about the topic?**

- **What else do you want to know about the subject?**

Fact vs. Opinion

- **Take a piece of paper and divide it in half.**

- **Write "Fact" and "Opinion" on the top of each half.**

- **Write all the facts and opinions from the text in each column.**

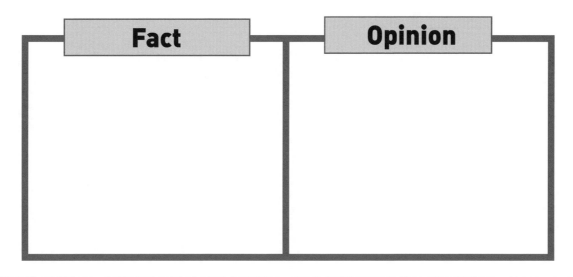

Fact	Opinion

Fact and Opinion with Expository Text

- **Make a chart like the one below.**

- **Find five facts from the text and write them down.**

- **Find five opinions from the text and write them down.**

- **On the back of your chart, explain in your own words what makes them facts and opinions.**

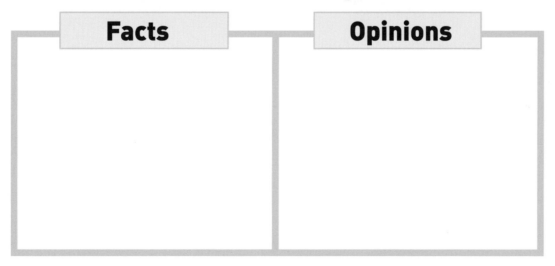

Facts	Opinions

Historical Fiction

- **Create a chart like the one below on a sheet of paper.**

- **Find examples in your story of fiction and non-fiction elements and fill in the chart.**

Fictional Elements	Non-Fictional Elements

How-To

● **List all the steps in the correct order that were used to make** _____ **that was discussed in the text.**

1

2

3

4

Illustrating the Story

Draw a picture to illustrate both the problem and solution in the text.

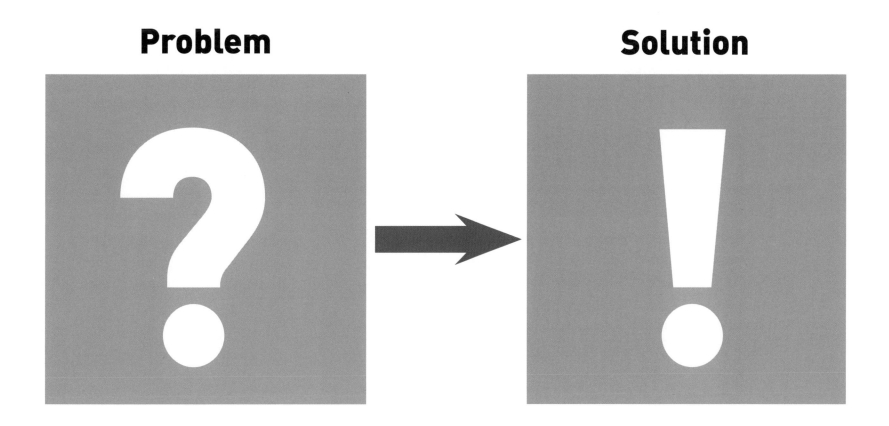

Information Illustrated

- **Draw a picture or diagram of the**

_____

  that was talked about in the text.

- **Label its parts.**

KWL Chart

- **Fill out the first two sections of the KWL chart *before* reading your text.**

- **When you are finished reading, fill out the last section.**

What I Know	What I Want to Know	What I Learned

KWL Variations

- **(KWLA) What I <u>KNOW</u>, what I <u>WANT</u> to know, what I <u>LEARNED</u>, how what I learned <u>AFFECTED</u> me**

- **(KWLP) What I <u>KNOW</u>, what I <u>WANT</u> to know, what I <u>LEARNED</u>, where is the <u>PAGE/PROOF</u> of what I learned**

Letter Writing

- **Write a letter to the main character.**

- **What would you ask the main character?**

- **What do you want to tell the main character?**

Main Character Cause and Effect

● **Using the main character as your guide, make a cause and effect story map like the one below.**

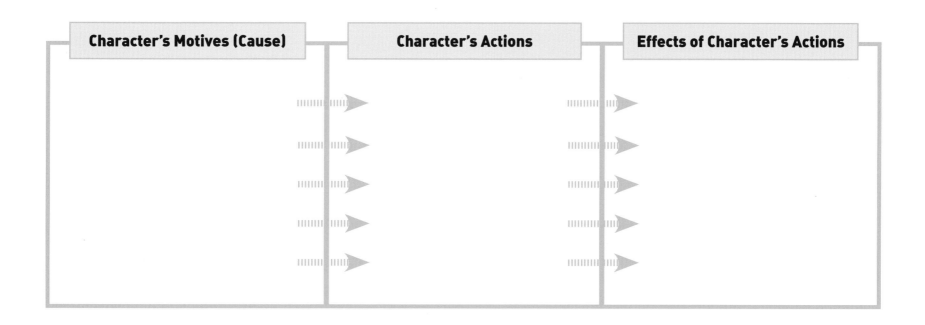

Character's Motives (Cause)	Character's Actions	Effects of Character's Actions

Main Idea

- **Who or what was the text about?**

- **What was the most important thing about the who or what of the text?**

- **Now take that information and write a *main idea* sentence about the text using as few words as you can.**

- **Draw a picture to go with your sentence.**

Narrative Story Structure

Answer these questions about your narrative story:

- **Who were the characters?**

- **What was the setting?**

- **What was the problem?**

- **How was the problem solved?**

Picture Vocabulary

Take a sheet of paper and fold it into eight squares. You may make more if you like.

● Find all the words from your text that were new or hard for you to understand and write them down (one word per square).

Draw a picture that helps you know what the word means.

● Write a definition in your own words that explains the meaning of the word.

● Use your text or a dictionary to help you.

Point of View

- **Rewrite the story from the**

  _____

  point of view.

- **How would the events of the story be different?**

Prediction

- **Think about how the story ended.**

- **What do you predict will happen next?**

- **Write and illustrate your prediction.**

Problem and Solution

- **Write down an important problem that was in the text.**

- **It was an important problem because**

  _____ .

- **List all the steps that were tried to solve the problem.**

- **The problem was finally solved when**

  _____ .

Questions to Main Idea

Answer these questions about your story. Next, use the information to write a main idea statement about the story.

Who? _____

Wanted? _____

But? _____

So? _____

Then? _____

Main Idea: _____

Reader's Response

Use the sentence stem your teacher checked to write a story response.

- ☐ I think...
- ☐ I wish...
- ☐ I wonder...
- ☐ I was surprised...
- ☐ This reminds me of...
- ☐ I feel...
- ☐ I'm confused about...
- ☐ I suppose...
- ☐ I can relate to...
- ☐ I remember...
- ☐ I like _____ part of the book because...
- ☐ This is like _____ story because...
- ☐ I noticed that...
- ☐ I like when the author said...
- ☐ This interests me because...
- ☐ This reminds me of _____ because...
- ☐ I like/dislike the book because...
- ☐ The setting of the story is important because...

- ☐ This reminds me of _____ that happened in my life.
- ☐ A question I have about the book so far is...
- ☐ If I were this character, I would...
- ☐ I didn't understand the part when...
- ☐ The most exciting part of the book was...
- ☐ This book reminds me of _____ book because...
- ☐ I agree/disagree with the author about...
- ☐ I question the accuracy of...
- ☐ Some important details I noticed were...
- ☐ I think the author wrote this book because...
- ☐ After the book ends, I predict...
- ☐ The author got me interested when...
- ☐ I learned...
- ☐ My feelings about the book changed when...
- ☐ The book helped me to...
- ☐ To summarize the text, I would say...
- ☐ The genre of this book is _____ because...

Realistic vs. Fantasy

- **Take a piece of paper and divide it in half.**

- **Write "Realistic" and "Fantasy" on the top of each half.**

- **Write events or themes from the story that fit under each side.**

Realistic	Fantasy

Recording Mental Images

- **Read to page _____ of your text.**

- **What image is in your head after reading?**

- **Capture the image in words and pictures in your reading journal or on a sheet of paper.**

- **Share your image with others. How do they compare?**

NOTE: This can be done as a listening comprehension activity after a teacher read aloud.

Retelling Important Narrative Events

- **Take a sheet of paper and make a retelling map like the one below.**

- **Write all the important events that happened in your narrative.**

- **Draw a picture to go with each event.**

Event 1

Event 2

Event 3

Event 4

Retelling Important Informational Facts

- **Take a sheet of paper and make a retelling map like the one below.**

- **Write all the important facts the author wanted you to know about the topic of the text.**

- **Draw a picture to go with each fact.**

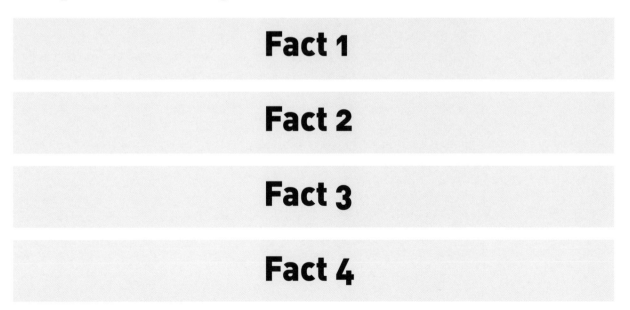

Fact 1

Fact 2

Fact 3

Fact 4

Sequencing

- **Write down four events that happened in the text on four index cards.**

- **Exchange the cards with your partner and see if he/she can arrange the cards in the correct order.**

- **Check yourself with the text.**

- **Take a sheet of paper and glue the cards to it in the correct order.**

- **Draw a picture to match each event.**

Setting

- **Where does most of the story take place?**

- **Draw a picture of the setting and describe it in your own words.**

Stop and Reflect

- On a sheet of paper or in your reading journal write down the page numbers your teacher has inserted here.

- These pages will be your "Stop and Reflect" points as you read the text.

- At every "Stop and Reflect" point, take a moment to jot down any thoughts you have about your reading and the text so far.

Stop and Reflect points for _____

Page _____	Page _____	Page _____
Page _____	Page _____	Page _____
Page _____	Page _____	Page _____

Story Map

- **Make a story map like the one below on a piece of paper.**

- **Write what happened and draw pictures to match.**

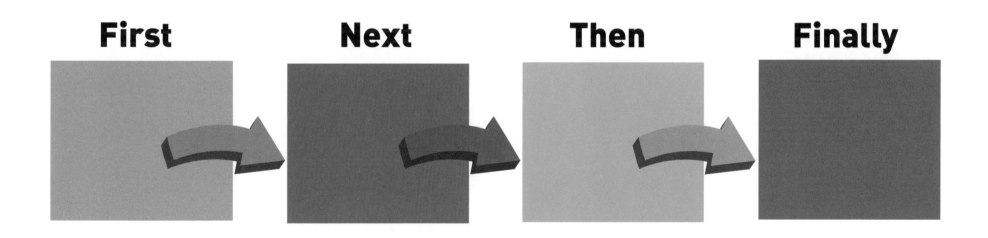

First   **Next**   **Then**   **Finally**

Story Map: Narrative Text

● **Make a narrative map like the one below and fill it in with the correct information from your story.**

Title and Author

Setting

Characters

Problem

Events

Solution

Story Summarization

- **Write a three-sentence summarization of the text.**

- **Write one sentence that tells about the beginning of the text, one that tells about the middle, and one that tells about the end of the text.**

Summary

Story Webbing

Fill in the web about your story.

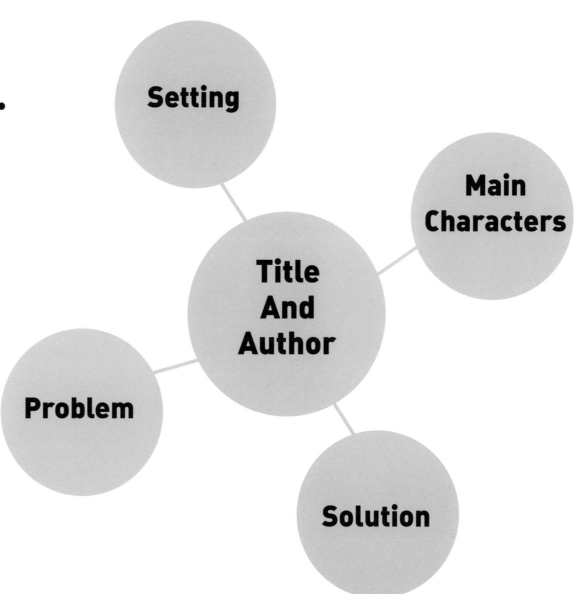

Text-to-Self Connections

- **Think about the text you just read and your own life.**

- **Was there something in the text that reminded you of your life?**

- **Write about it.**

Text-to-Text Connections

- **Think about the text you just read and other stories or books you have read.**

- **Was there something in the text that reminded you of another text?**

- **Write about it.**

Text-to-World Connections

- **Think about the text you just read and the world.**

- **Was there something in the text that reminded you of something happening in the world?**

- **Write about it.**

The Best Part

- **Pick your favorite part of the text and describe it.**

- **Next, explain in your own words why it is your favorite part.**

- **Draw a picture to go with it.**

The 5 Ws ... Plus H

- **On a piece of paper answer these questions about your text:**

Who?

What?

When?

Where?

Why?

How?

Timeline

- **Make a timeline of the events in the text.**

- **Use time phrases or dates used in the text as a guide.**

Morning

Afternoon

Evening

The next day

Two weeks later

Use Your Text to Complete the Diagram

(either write or draw it)

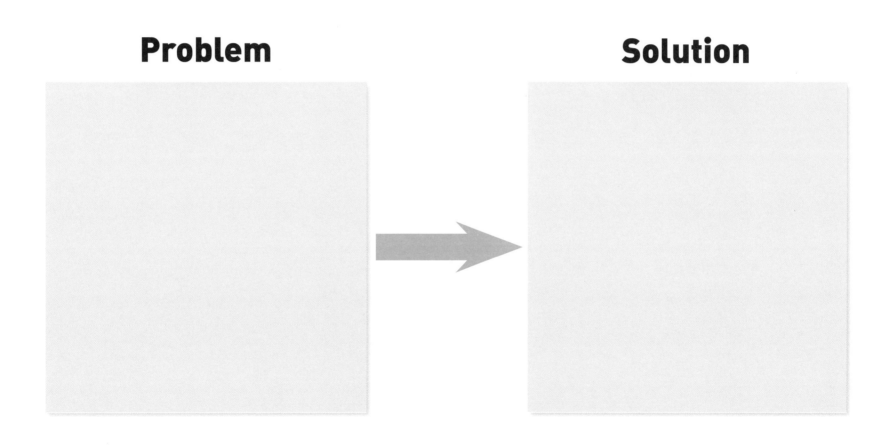

Problem

Solution

Vocabulary Inferences

Make a chart like the one below.

● Write down words from your text that are tricky or hard to understand.

● In the middle section, write what you infer the word means.

In the last section, write what helped you to make that inference.

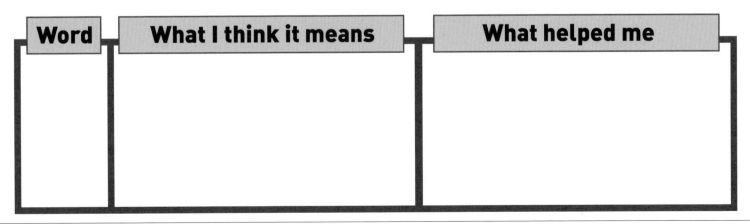

Word	What I think it means	What helped me

Vocabulary Square

- **Pick a word from the text that was new or hard for you to understand. Make a Vocabulary Square.**

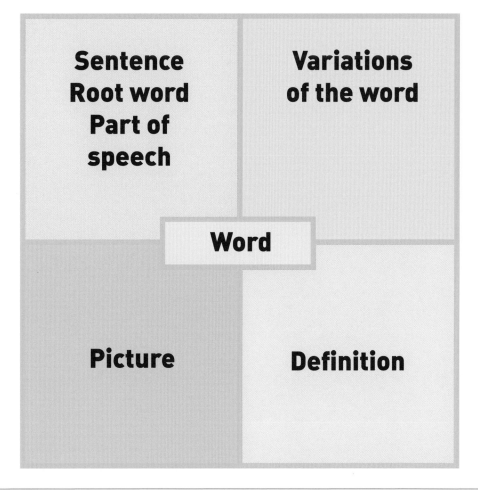

Webbing

1. **Make a web like the one here about your story.**

2. **Fill in the necessary information for each section.**

3. **Next, use the information to write a main idea statement about the story.**

4. **Draw a picture to match the main idea.**

Who

Why

Title

What

Where

When

What Do You Want to Know?

- Make a chart like the one below.

- Think about the text you are about to read.

- What is one important question you have that you hope the text will answer? Write it in the first box.

- After reading the text, write and draw how the question was answered. Include the page number where you discovered the answer.

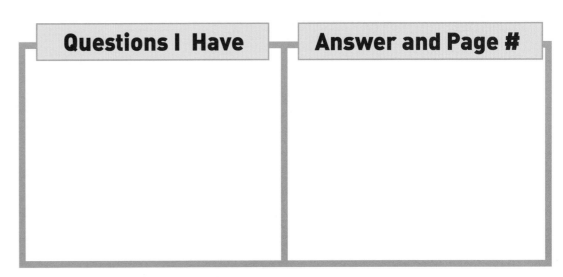

Questions I Have	Answer and Page #

Word Map

- **Pick a word that was new or hard for you to understand and make a Word Map.**

What is it?

WORD

What are some examples?

Non-examples

What is it like?

References

Boyles, Nancy N. *Constructing Meaning Through Kid-Friendly Comprehension Strategy Instruction*. Gainesville, FL: Maupin House, 2004.

Burke, Jim. *Reading Reminders: Tools, Tips, and Techniques*. Portsmouth, NH: Boynton/Cook Publishers, Inc., 2000.

Calkins, Lucy McCormick. *The Art of Teaching Reading.* New York: Longman, 2001.

"Comprehension Instruction: Texas Reading Initiative." Texas Education Agency, 2000.

Fountas, Irene, Gay Su Pinnell. *Guiding Readers & Writers (Grades 3-6): Teaching Comprehension, Genre, and Content Literacy.* Portsmouth, NH: Heinemann, 2000.

—. *Guided Reading: Good First Teaching for All Children.* Portsmouth, NH: Heinemann, 1996.

Goudvis, Anne, Stephanie Harvey. *Strategies That Work: Teaching Comprehension to Enhance Understanding.* York, ME: Stenhouse Publishers, 2000.

Heimlich, Joan E., Susan D. Pittleman. *Semantic Mapping: Classroom Applications.* Newark, DE: International Reading Association, 1986.

Keene, Ellen Oliver, Susan Zimmerman. *Mosaic of Thought: Teaching Comprehension in a Reader's Workshop.* Portsmouth, NH: Heinemann, 1997.

Miller, Debbie. *Reading with Meaning: Teaching Comprehension in the Primary Grades.* Portland, ME: Stenhouse Publishers, 2002.

"Promoting Vocabulary Development: Texas Reading Initiative," Texas Education Agency, 2000.

Stahl, S.A., S.J. Vancil. "Discussion is What Makes Semantic Maps Work." *The Reading Teacher.* vol. 40: 62-67, 1986.

Stauffer, Russell G. *Directing the Reading-Thinking Process.* New York: Harper and Row, 1975.

Taberski, Sharon. *On Solid Ground: Strategies for Teaching Reading K-3.* Portsmouth, NH: Heinemann, 2000.

Zike, Dinah. *Big Book of Books and Activities.* San Antonio, TX: Dinah-Might Activities, 1992.

About the Author

Emily Cayuso is a campus instructional coordinator/reading specialist in San Antonio, Texas. She has taught a variety of primary grades and has worked as a reading recovery and Title 1 reading teacher specialist for more than thirty years. Emily has also served as a part-time adjunct faculty member at the University of Texas in San Antonio, working with pre-service teachers. She conducts workshops for reading and language arts teachers. Recognized twice in "Who's Who Among America's Teachers," Emily is the author of *Designing Teacher Study Groups: A Guide for Success*, *Flip for Comprehension* and its Spanish translation, *Dar la Vuelta a la Comprensión, Flip for Word Work*, and *Flip for Non-Fiction Comprehension*. She holds a B.S. and an M.Ed.